Dear Parents and Educators,

Welcome to Penguin Young Readers! As parents and educators, you know that each child develops at his or her own pace—in terms of speech, critical thinking, and, of course, reading. Penguin Young Readers recognizes this fact. As a result, each Penguin Young Readers book is assigned a traditional easy-to-read level (1–4) as well as a Guided Reading Level (A–P). Both of these systems will help you choose the right book for your child. Please refer to the back of each book for specific leveling information. Penguin Young Readers features esteemed authors and illustrators, stories about favorite characters, fascinating nonfiction, and more!

## The Tale of Beatrix Potter

**LEVEL 4**

GUIDED READING LEVEL **N**

This book is perfect for a **Fluent Reader** who:
- can read the text quickly with minimal effort;
- has good comprehension skills;
- can self-correct (can recognize when something doesn't sound right); and
- can read aloud smoothly and with expression.

Here are some **activities** you can do during and after reading this book:
- Nonfiction: Nonfiction books deal with facts and events that are real. Talk about the elements of nonfiction. Discuss some of the facts you learned about Beatrix Potter. For example, you now know that Beatrix had a lot of pets growing up.
- Creative Writing: You read about Beatrix Potter, an author and illustrator who was inspired by the people, animals, and countryside around her. Now it's your turn to write a story of your own. Use the following prompts to get started:
  - What's your favorite animal?
  - If this animal could talk, what would he or she say?
  - What does this animal like to do during the day?

Remember, sharing the love of reading with a child is the best gift you can give!

—Bonnie Bader, EdM
  Penguin Young Readers program

*Penguin Young Readers are leveled by independent reviewers applying the standards developed by Irene Fountas and Gay Su Pinnell in *Matching Books to Readers: Using Leveled Books in Guided Reading*, Heinemann, 1999.

PENGUIN YOUNG READERS
An Imprint of Penguin Random House LLC

Photo credits: cover, page 3 (photo of Beatrix Potter), page 10, page 41: courtesy of the Victoria and Albert Museum; page 3 (illustrations), page 4, page 6, page 7, page 17, page 22, page 25, page 26, pages 28–29, page 31, page 34, page 36, page 38, page 42, page 43, pages 44–45: courtesy of Frederick Warne & Co.; page 5, page 8, page 11, page 19, page 20, page 21 (top and bottom), page 24, page 30, page 32, page 33, page 35, page 39, page 46, page 48: © Frederick Warne & Co., 2002; page 9, page 40: courtesy of the National Trust; page 12, page 14: courtesy of Frederick Warne & Co. and the Linder Collection; page 13, page 15, page 16, page 23: courtesy of Frederick Warne & Co. and the Victoria and Albert Museum; page 18: courtesy of Pearson PLC; page 27, page 47: courtesy of a private collector.

Text copyright © 2016 by Frederick Warne & Co. All rights reserved. Published by Penguin Young Readers, an imprint of Penguin Random House LLC, 345 Hudson Street, New York, New York 10014. Manufactured in China.

Library of Congress Cataloging-in-Publication Data is available.

ISBN 978-0-241-24937-6 (pbk)                    10 9 8 7 6 5 4 3 2 1
ISBN 978-0-241-24954-3 (hc)                     10 9 8 7 6 5 4 3 2 1

PENGUIN YOUNG READERS

LEVEL

FLUENT
READER

4

# THE TALE OF BEATRIX POTTER

adapted by Sara Schonfeld

Penguin Young Readers
An Imprint of Penguin Random House

The year was 1893. A young woman was traveling by train.

She had a covered basket. Inside that basket was a rabbit called Peter.

Peter Piper the rabbit went everywhere with her. She even walked him on a leash!

No one could have guessed that Peter was going to be a very famous rabbit one day. His owner was going to be famous, too. Her name was Beatrix Potter.

Beatrix Potter was born in London in 1866. Her parents were rich. They had a big house and servants.

Beatrix spent a lot of time at home with her nanny. She did not meet many other children.

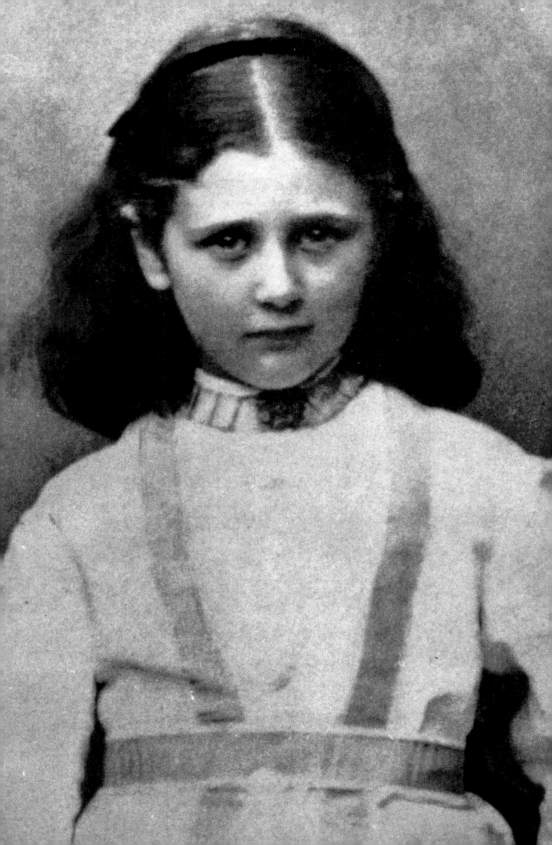

When Beatrix was six years old, her

brother, Bertram, was born. Finally,

she had someone to play with!

Beatrix and her brother both loved animals. The family had a dog named Spot, but that wasn't enough for the children.

They sneaked all kinds of animals into their room. When the family took vacations, Beatrix and Bertram would bring back new pets. There were rabbits, mice, lizards, bats, birds, and frogs. Once they even got a snake—and it escaped!

Beatrix's parents sent her brother away to school when he was 11. They had a teacher come to the house to teach Beatrix. Not going to school meant it was hard for Beatrix to meet other kids her age. She was sad. And lonely.

So the animals became her friends. She loved drawing and painting them. Every day Beatrix couldn't wait for her lessons to end so she could go back to her art!

When Beatrix was 19 years old, she finished her lessons at home. Now she had more time to draw and paint.

Everyone liked her art. Her uncle said she should try selling it. Beatrix liked that idea.

15

Soon Beatrix sold her art! She
drew six Christmas cards of
a rabbit family.

A happy New Year to you.

Beatrix was excited to sell her art,
but she wanted to sell stories, too.

A few years later, Beatrix had the chance to share her writing. She wrote a story in a letter. She even drew pictures to go along with the story. The rabbit in the story was named Peter. Just like her pet!

Eastwood Dunkeld
Sep 4. 93

My dear Noel,
I don't know what to write to you, so I shall tell you a story about four little rabbits. whose names were–

Flopsy, Mopsy Cottontail

and Peter

They lived with their mother in a sand bank under the root of a big fir tree.

After reading the letter, Beatrix's old teacher told her that she should try writing a children's book.

That letter about four little rabbits became a longer story. This was *The Tale of Peter Rabbit.*

but Peter – who was very
naughty – ran straight
away to Mr McGregor's
garden

Beatrix sent it to six publishers.
But no one wanted to turn her story
about Peter Rabbit into a real book.
Beatrix did not give up. She decided
to pay a printer to make the books.

Here comes Peter with the Post-bag! — "Is this the right rabbit hole, please?"

And 250 copies of her book were
printed. They sold out. She had to
make more!

Then a publishing company agreed to publish the book. They made 8,000 copies. And they sold out!

Now the publisher wanted more books. So Beatrix wrote more stories about other animals. Finally, she was a published author! Beatrix was very happy.

THE TALE OF
PETER RABBIT

BY
BEATRIX POTTER

F·WARNE & C°.

She was also happy because a young man named Norman Warne asked her to marry him. Norman was the editor of Beatrix's books.

Beatrix wanted to marry Norman. Her parents didn't like the idea. But Beatrix was almost 40 years old! She decided she was old enough to make her own decisions.

She also had enough money to buy her own house. She bought a farm in England in a beautiful place called the Lake District.

Unfortunately, Beatrix's happiness did not last. Norman got sick and died. Beatrix was very sad.

Beatrix never forgot Norman. But her new house, friends, and work helped her to feel happy again.

Her characters were becoming very popular. Soon there were Peter Rabbit dolls, Peter Rabbit wallpapers, and Peter Rabbit board games!

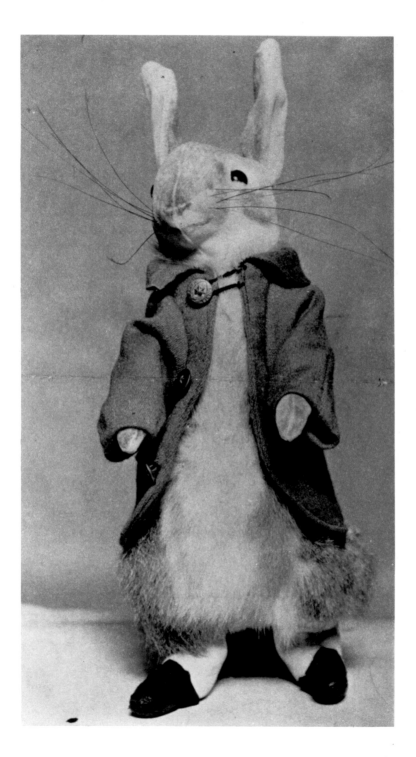

While she was writing, Beatrix always thought about her young readers. When she wrote *The Tale of Timmy Tiptoes*, she added a gray squirrel and a bear for her American readers.

Beatrix also drew pictures of houses and shops from her new neighborhood in her books.

In fact, she loved the Lake District so much that she wanted to help protect it.

Lots of people were knocking down old farms. They were building on farmland. Beatrix wanted to make sure the Lake District stayed the way it was. She liked the farms and the plants and the animals.

Beatrix bought more land there. This way, she could make sure the land wouldn't be destroyed or changed.

As time passed, Beatrix realized that her parents were getting older. Beatrix worried about them . . . and they worried about her!

In 1912, a man named William Heelis asked Beatrix to marry him. Her parents didn't like him. Once again, Beatrix knew that she could decide for herself. But she wanted her parents to be happy, too.

Beatrix's brother, Bertram, decided it was time to tell his parents a secret. He had been married for 11 years and had never told them! Maybe this made Beatrix's plan to marry William less surprising. Her parents said it was okay for them to marry.

Beatrix and William married in October 1913.

Both Beatrix and her husband were very happy in the countryside. Beatrix became a real countrywoman. She farmed. She won prizes for her sheep.

41

Beatrix had always loved animals
and children. She wanted to help
them. So, she drew greeting cards to
help raise money for sick kids, and
she kept buying more land to protect
in the Lake District.

Same size carefully vignetted

As she got older, Beatrix found that she couldn't go outside very much.

Luckily, she could remember
the flowers and animals she once
saw outside.

After she got sick in 1943, Beatrix died. She was 77.

She left 15 farms to the National Trust. They would protect the land. They make sure no one can knock down the farmhouses or build new ones. They also keep the plants and animals safe.

Beatrix's stories are still being published all over the world. New children enjoy the books every year. We are lucky that Beatrix wrote about that rabbit named Peter so we can still read about him today.